D0185830

I Can Draw...
PEOPLE

Artwork by Terry Longhurst

Text by Amanda O'Neill

p

This is a Parragon Book
This edition published in 2003

Parragon
Queen Street House
4 Queen Street
Bath BA1 1HE, UK

Copyright © Parragon 2001

Designed, packaged, and produced by
Touchstone

All rights reserved. No part of this publication may be reproduced, stored
in a retrieval system, or transmitted in any way or by any means, electronic,
mechanical, photocopying, recording or otherwise, without the prior
permission of the copyright holder.

Hardback: ISBN 1-40540-354-3
Paperback: ISBN 1-40540-038-2

Artwork by Terry Longhurst
Text by Amanda O'Neill
Edited by Philip de Ste. Croix

Printed in Dubai,U.A.E

About this book

Everybody can enjoy drawing, but sometimes it's hard to know where to begin. The subject you want to draw can look very complicated. This book shows you how to start, by breaking down your subject into a series of simple shapes.

The tools you need are very simple. The basic requirements are paper and pencils. Very thin paper wears through if you have to rub out a line, so choose paper that is thick enough to work on. Pencils come with different leads, from very hard to very soft. Very hard pencils give a clean, thin line which is best for finishing drawings. Very soft ones give a thicker, darker line. You will probably find a medium pencil most useful.

If you want to colour in your drawing, you have the choice of paints, coloured inks, or felt-tip pens. Fine felt-tips are useful for drawing outlines, thick felt-tips are better for colouring in.

The most important tool you have is your own eyes. The mistake many people make is to draw what they think something looks like, instead of really looking at it carefully first. Half the secret of making your drawing look good is getting the proportions right. Study your subject before you start, and break it down in your mind into sections. Check how much bigger, or longer, or shorter, one part is than another. Notice where one part joins another, and at what angle. See where there are flowing curves, and where there are straight lines.

The step-by-step drawings in this book show you exactly how to do this. Each subject is broken down into easy stages, so you can build up your drawing one piece at a time. Look carefully at each shape before – and after – you draw it. If you find you have drawn it the wrong size or in the wrong place, correct it before you go on. Then the next shape will fit into place, and piece-by-piece you can build up a fantastic picture.

Cowboy

From about 1870 onwards, cattle raising was big business in the Wild West of America – and it all depended on cowboys. They tended the herds, and drove them long distances to markets. Western films make their lives look glamorous, but they worked hard in tough conditions.

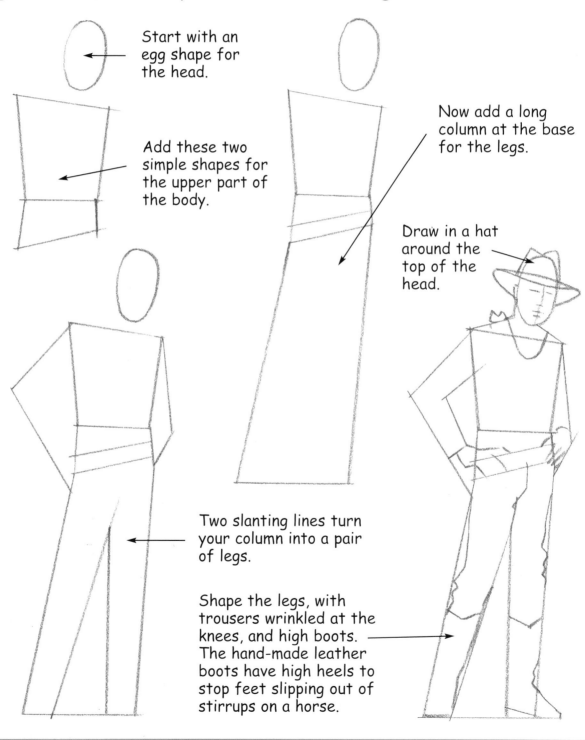

Start with an egg shape for the head.

Add these two simple shapes for the upper part of the body.

Now add a long column at the base for the legs.

Draw in a hat around the top of the head.

Two slanting lines turn your column into a pair of legs.

Shape the legs, with trousers wrinkled at the knees, and high boots. The hand-made leather boots have high heels to stop feet slipping out of stirrups on a horse.

A line sketched down the centre of the face will help you position eyes, nose and mouth.

Now draw in his clothes – jeans, shirt and a short waistcoat, or 'vest'.

A gun was protection from thieves and rustlers (cattle thieves). But long months on the trail made for short tempers, and gunfights were common.

The gunbelt is worn low on the hips, at a slant. The six-shooter gun is carried in a leather holster.

A bandanna (cotton neckcloth) protects his neck from the Sun. On cattle drives, it serves as a mask against the choking dust kicked up by the animals' feet.

The holster is tied to the thigh with a cord to stop it moving about.

The high, broad-rimmed hat keeps the head cool and shades the eyes from the Sun.

There are still cowboys today – but they tend their cattle from pick-up trucks and helicopters as well as from horses as in days gone by.

Japanese Girl

This Japanese girl is wearing her traditional costume, a loose, long-sleeved gown called a kimono. This graceful garment is worn both by men and women. The wide sash at the waist, called an obi, is also traditional.

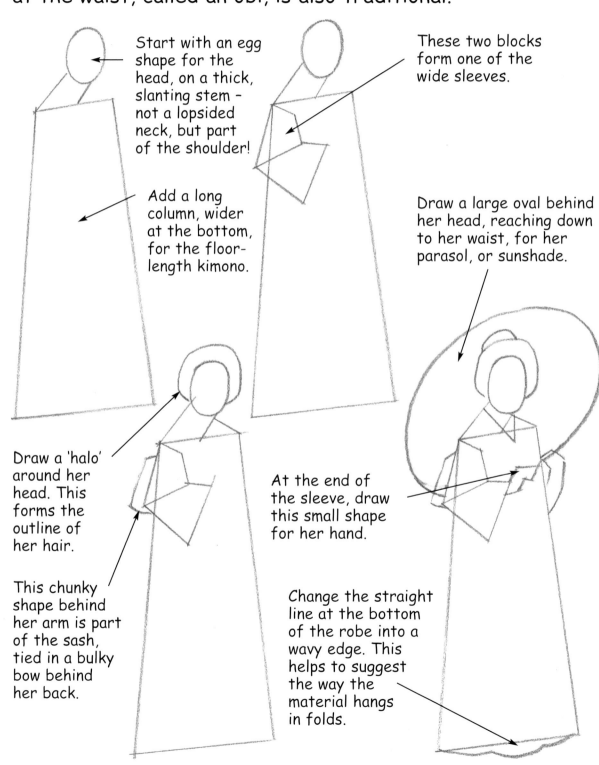

Start with an egg shape for the head, on a thick, slanting stem – not a lopsided neck, but part of the shoulder!

Add a long column, wider at the bottom, for the floor-length kimono.

These two blocks form one of the wide sleeves.

Draw a large oval behind her head, reaching down to her waist, for her parasol, or sunshade.

Draw a 'halo' around her head. This forms the outline of her hair.

This chunky shape behind her arm is part of the sash, tied in a bulky bow behind her back.

At the end of the sleeve, draw this small shape for her hand.

Change the straight line at the bottom of the robe into a wavy edge. This helps to suggest the way the material hangs in folds.

Draw in the slender ribs of her delicate paper parasol.

A folded fan is held in her right hand, ready for graceful use.

Her kimono hangs in soft folds, shown by pencil lines. Be sure to match these up with the curves of the hem.

Ink in the parasol struts lightly. When you colour in your drawing, you may want to add painted leaves or flowers on the open sunshade.

The obi (sash) is often beautifully embroidered.

Nowadays, more and more Japanese wear Western-style clothing rather than beautiful kimonos like this.

She wears a simple sandal, and a divided sock which separates the big toe from the other toes.

Tennis Player

The game of tennis was developed in 15th century France when it was played indoors. The outdoors version, lawn tennis, became popular in the 19th century, when the modern rules were drawn up.

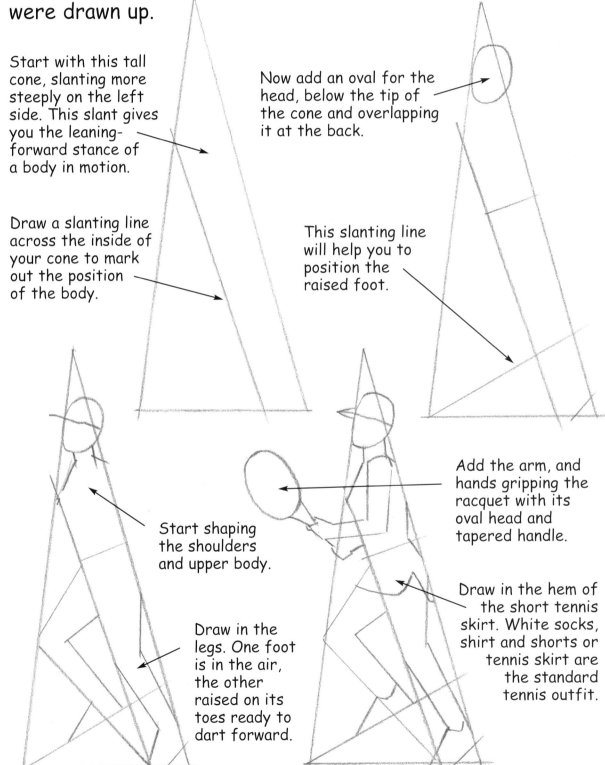

Start with this tall cone, slanting more steeply on the left side. This slant gives you the leaning-forward stance of a body in motion.

Draw a slanting line across the inside of your cone to mark out the position of the body.

Now add an oval for the head, below the tip of the cone and overlapping it at the back.

This slanting line will help you to position the raised foot.

Start shaping the shoulders and upper body.

Draw in the legs. One foot is in the air, the other raised on its toes ready to dart forward.

Add the arm, and hands gripping the racquet with its oval head and tapered handle.

Draw in the hem of the short tennis skirt. White socks, shirt and shorts or tennis skirt are the standard tennis outfit.

Draw in the face and hair.

A baseball cap shades the player's eyes from the Sun.

Start to ink in your outlines carefully.

Early racquet frames were made of wood, often ash. Nowadays modern materials like fibreglass or carbon graphite are used.

Tennis shoes support the ankles and cushion the soles of the feet.

Draw the racquet strings with fine, criss-crossed lines.

The most famous tennis championships in the world are the All-England Championships held at Wimbledon. They were first played there in 1877.

Inline Skater

Ice skates were known in ancient times. Roller skates arrived in the 18th century, fitted with wheels to glide over the ground instead of blades for skating on ice. They soon became popular worldwide. Inline skates were a 1980s development, faster and easier to turn.

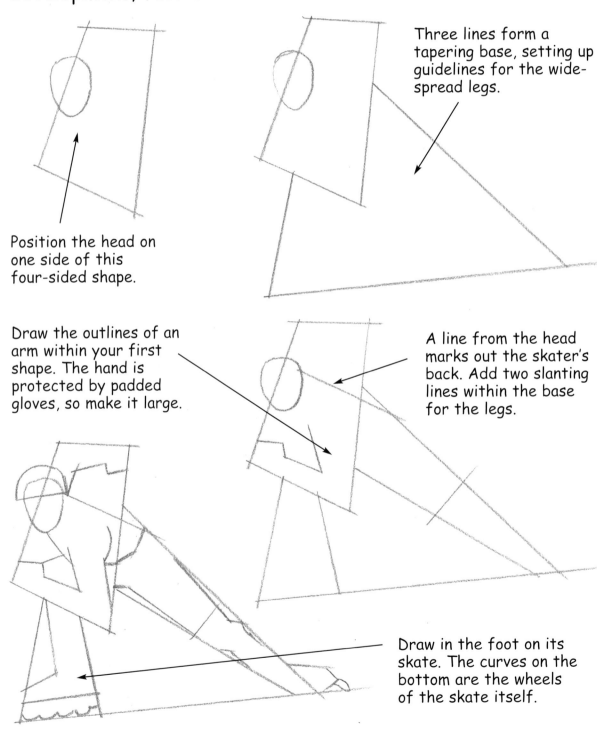

Three lines form a tapering base, setting up guidelines for the wide-spread legs.

Position the head on one side of this four-sided shape.

Draw the outlines of an arm within your first shape. The hand is protected by padded gloves, so make it large.

A line from the head marks out the skater's back. Add two slanting lines within the base for the legs.

Draw in the foot on its skate. The curves on the bottom are the wheels of the skate itself.

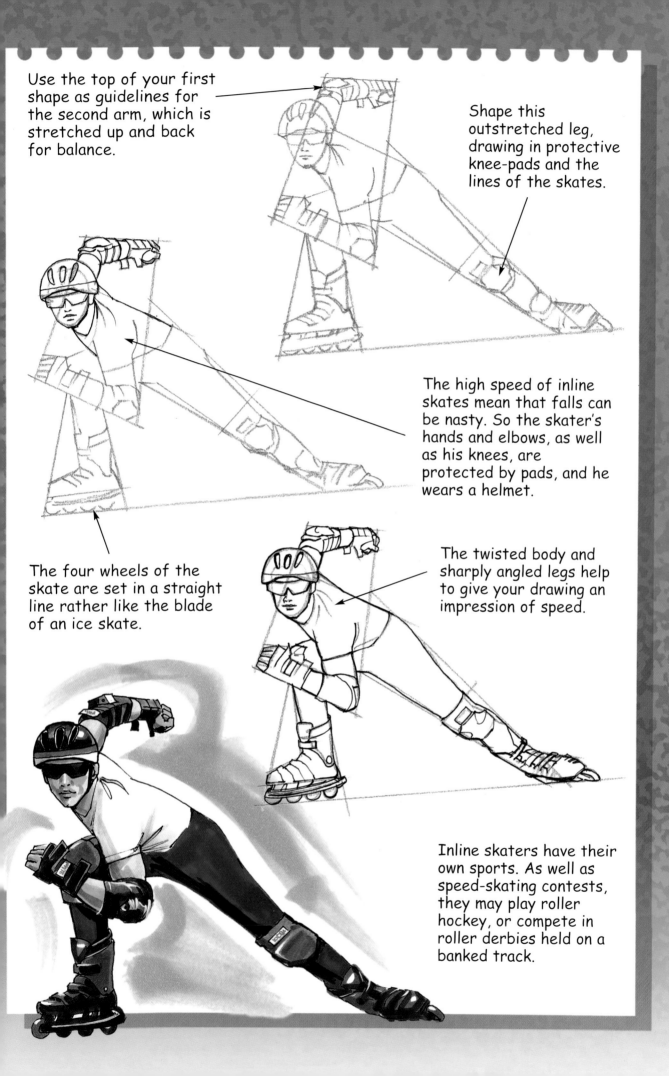

Use the top of your first shape as guidelines for the second arm, which is stretched up and back for balance.

Shape this outstretched leg, drawing in protective knee-pads and the lines of the skates.

The high speed of inline skates mean that falls can be nasty. So the skater's hands and elbows, as well as his knees, are protected by pads, and he wears a helmet.

The four wheels of the skate are set in a straight line rather like the blade of an ice skate.

The twisted body and sharply angled legs help to give your drawing an impression of speed.

Inline skaters have their own sports. As well as speed-skating contests, they may play roller hockey, or compete in roller derbies held on a banked track.

Guardsman

Guards troops started out as the personal bodyguards of royalty. Today, the Guards are the 'crack' regiments of the British Army. This soldier is a member of the Household Cavalry and would be mounted on horseback for ceremonial occasions.

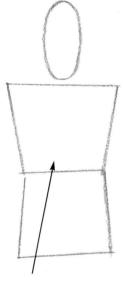

Draw the body in two sections, divided at the waist.

All Guardsmen have to be tall, and the helmet with its crest and horsehair plume adds to their height.

Draw in the arms. The hands are clasped together at waist level where they rest on the Guardsman's sword.

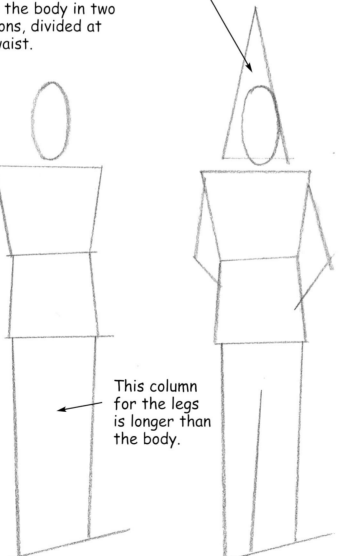

This column for the legs is longer than the body.

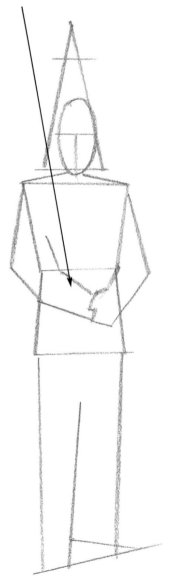

Start drawing in the sash, epaulettes (shoulder decorations) and other details of the uniform.

A moustache, though not essential, is part of military tradition. At one time, French hussars unable to grow a moustache had to paint one on with boot polish!

The hands, in long gloves called gauntlets, rest on the hilt of the sword.

Add some wavy edges to make the sleeves and trouser legs look more realistic.

Uniform decorations are often reminders of old customs. For example, the cord down the centre of the shoulder belt, now only decorative, used to carry a powder flask for priming guns.

A magnificent formal uniform like this is only worn on special occasions, like the Trooping The Colour celebrations on the Queen's birthday.

The long boots reach the thighs. They are called Wellingtons after the Duke of Wellington, who introduced them.

Inuit Hunter

The Inuit are people of the Arctic – the icy land around the North Pole that is one of the harshest regions of the world. For thousands of years they have lived by hunting and fishing. They made skin tents for summer use, and houses of stone or even snow blocks (igloos) for winter.

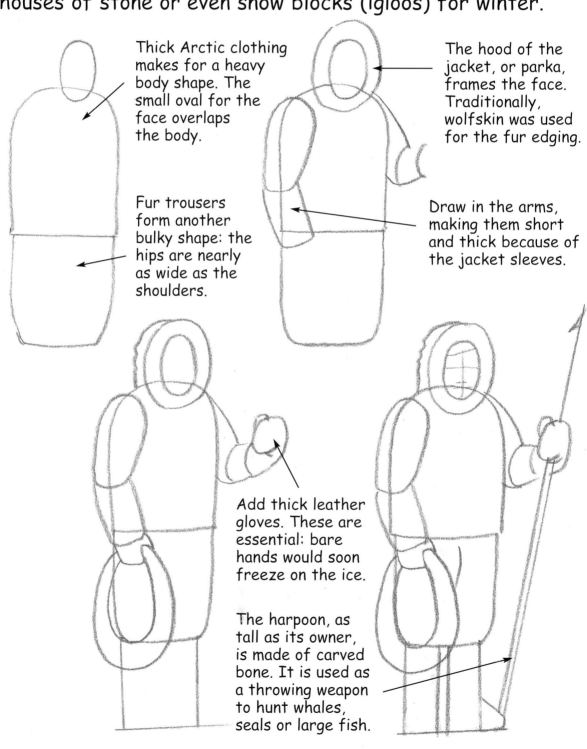

Thick Arctic clothing makes for a heavy body shape. The small oval for the face overlaps the body.

Fur trousers form another bulky shape: the hips are nearly as wide as the shoulders.

The hood of the jacket, or parka, frames the face. Traditionally, wolfskin was used for the fur edging.

Draw in the arms, making them short and thick because of the jacket sleeves.

Add thick leather gloves. These are essential: bare hands would soon freeze on the ice.

The harpoon, as tall as its owner, is made of carved bone. It is used as a throwing weapon to hunt whales, seals or large fish.

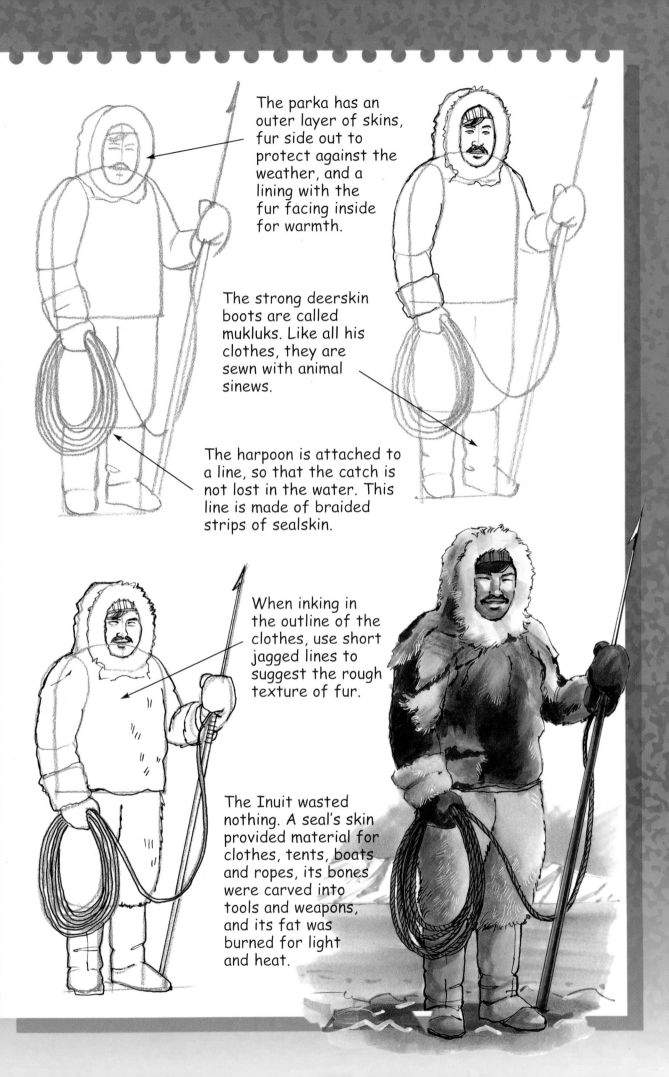

The parka has an outer layer of skins, fur side out to protect against the weather, and a lining with the fur facing inside for warmth.

The strong deerskin boots are called mukluks. Like all his clothes, they are sewn with animal sinews.

The harpoon is attached to a line, so that the catch is not lost in the water. This line is made of braided strips of sealskin.

When inking in the outline of the clothes, use short jagged lines to suggest the rough texture of fur.

The Inuit wasted nothing. A seal's skin provided material for clothes, tents, boats and ropes, its bones were carved into tools and weapons, and its fat was burned for light and heat.